THE ULTIMATE BBQ GUIDE INCLUDES MARINADES, RUBS, SAUCES, MEAT, POULTRY, FISH, SIDES AND SALAD RECIPES.

Disclaimer

Contents

Introduction

Out of all the cooking methods that exist, barbecue is one of the most flavorful. Nothing compares to the mouth-watering taste of a juicy grilled steak or smoked baby-back ribs. For all of its flavor, however, barbecue is a fairly simple cooking method. There are several different types of barbecue, but they all involve some kind of flame – that is where the depth of flavor comes from. Two of the most popular types of barbecue include grilling and smoking.

Grilling vs. Smoking

When it comes to barbecue, you have two main cooking methods to choose from: grilling and smoking. Grilling involves intense, more direct heat and shorter cooking times while smoking involves indirect heat and longer cooking times. Smoking is often associated with the phrase "low and slow" because you cook the meat at low temperatures (around 200°F to 250°F) over a long period of time, often several hours. With grilling you use higher temperatures (around 400°F to 500°F) for shorter cook times, generally less than an hour.

There are two different types of grilling – gas and charcoal. Gas grills use propane to produce flames while charcoal grills burn charcoal. The benefit of a gas grill is that it only takes a few seconds to light it – most grills come with an ignitor so you don't have to use matches. Charcoal grills take a little longer to prepare because you have to light the coals then give them time to heat up. The benefit of a charcoal grill is that you can achieve higher cooking temperatures, up to 700°F, and the smoke from the charcoal imparts a unique depth of flavor you can't achieve with a gas grill. The downside of charcoal is that it takes time to prepare and it is messier to clean up than gas.

Preparing the Flame

To ensure the maximum depth of flavor for your barbecue, you need to prepare your flame properly. Methods of flame preparation vary depending whether you are using a gas grill, a charcoal grill, or a smoker. <u>Below you will find tips for using all three barbecue methods</u>:

Gas Grill – Before you use your grill, it is recommended that you turn it on to high heat for 10 to 15 minutes or so – this will help to burn off any residue left from your last use. Then, simply adjust the heat according to your recipe. Searing food over direct flame ensures a tasty grilled flavor while cooking over indirect heat (only half the burners turned on) is ideal for whole chickens and large roasts.

Charcoal Grill – The easiest way to prepare a charcoal grill is to use a chimney starter. Fill the chimney with charcoal then place a few sheets of crumpled paper in the receptacle at the bottom. Light the newspaper and wait for flames to start coming out the top of the chimney (about 10 minutes). When they do, pour the charcoal into the grill then spread them out and give them another 15 minutes to heat up before you start grilling.

Smoker – To prepare your smoker you'll have to line the bottom with charcoal then light it and let the fire burn down. Adjust the vents on your smoker to stabilize the temperature – somewhere between 200°F and 240°F is best. Next, add hot water to the water pan and throw in some smoker wood. Once you've done this you can add the meat to the smoker and let it cook for the required length of time, checking the smoker frequently to make sure it maintains the right temperature.

Now that you understand the basics of barbecue, including the different types, you are probably eager to try them for yourself! If you are excited to give barbecue a shot, pick one of the delicious recipes included in this book to get started. In this book you will find a vast collection of barbecue recipes including rubs, marinades, chicken, meat, and fish. No matter what kind of barbecue you prefer, you will find a collection of tasty recipes ready to go. So what are you waiting for? Get cooking!

Benefits of Barbequing

*Grilling or chargrilling on a BBQ injects the food with wonderful smokey flavors. You also need to use less fatty and sugar sauces. A light dry rub with no oil can be used on almost any cut of lean meat before leaving to marinade and cooking on a hot BBQ / grill.

*It is quick! You can leave the meat / veggies to marinade over night and once the BBQ is hot enough the meat will cut in a very short period, making this a time friendly way to make lunch or dinner.

*It's sociable and gets you outside. Dine outside also, you will have less distractions like TV's and you will enjoy your food more. It promotes eating slower which can help portion control.

*It's super healthy - no processed foods allowed near a BBQ. With minimal preparation and quick cooking you can have a healthy but tasty meal that all the family will love.

*The variety is endless, if you have a picky eater in the family and all too often have to make two, if not three different dishes for dinner the BBQ will be your savour. You can cook a range

of meats AND veggies on the BBQ at the same time so this
also saves on washing up!

Marinades

Teriyaki

This is a zingy marinade perfect for pork, chicken and beef.
Pour over the meat and allow to marinade overnight.

Ingredients:

¼ cup soy sauce
2 tbsp teriyaki sauce
3 tsp freshly grated ginger
2 cloves garlic – crushed
2 tbsp soft brown sugar
¼ cup chicken stock
2-3 tbsp sweet sherry

Mix all the ingredients together in a food processor or blender
and whizz - pour over your meat, turn the meat occasionally
and keep covered so it doesn't dry out.

Spiced Yogurt Marinade

This is delicious Indian marinade and goes especially well on chicken and lamb, it really tenderizes and gives the meat a nice crust once cooked.

Ingredients:
1 cup yogurt (I like Greek)
¾ tsp ground cumin
¾ tsp ground cilantro (coriander)
¾ tsp cinnamon
1 garlic clove – crushed
1 tsp turmeric
1 tsp chili powder

Combine all the ingredients together in a bowl until mixed through. Pour over the meat ensuring it is all coated. Marinade for 4-24 hours. Keep meat covered in the fridge.

Garlic and Lemon

This marinade is great with lamb or chicken. I love to put this on a spatchcock chicken as it really seeps in to every part.

Ingredients:
2 tbsp lemon juice
2 tsp lemon rind
1 garlic clove – crushed
¼ cup white wine
¼ cup olive oil
2 tbsp brown sugar
1 tbsp freshly chopped lemon thyme
1 tbsp freshly chopped rosemary

Combine all the ingredients in a food processor and whizz until smooth. A hand whisk will to the same job but will just take a little longer.

Mustard and Herb

This works best with beef or lamb and gives the meat such an aromatic, intense flavour!

Ingredients:
¼ cup olive oil
2 tbsp balsamic vinegar
3 tsp Dijon mustard
2 tsp mixed dried herbs
2 tsp soft brown sugar
1 tbsp freshly ground parsley
Salt & Pepper to taste

Combine all the ingredients in a blender and whizz until you have an emulsion. Pour over the meat, cover and refrigerate. Turn the meat occasionally, marinade for up to 24 hours.

Chili & Lime

This marinade is good for fish but especially great for king prawns.

Ingredients:
Small bunch of fresh coriander - chopped
1 fresh red chili - deseeded and chopped
4 tbsp fresh lime juice
3 tbsp extra virgin olive oil
1 tbsp sesame oil
1 tbsp soy sauce
1 tsp soft brown sugar
1 clove of garlic - crushed

Mix all the ingredients in a blender. Marinade the prawns before placing on to wooden skewers and pour over any remaining marinade before cooking. The prawns do not need long to marinade as the acid in the lime will start to cook them, 3-5 minutes will be long enough.

Cajun

I make two versions of this marinade and I have to say it is quite possibly the easiest marinade ever if you have Cajun spices premade or have a jar of store bought Cajun seasoning.

.

Ingredients
¼ cup olive oil
2 tbsp Cajun spices (more or little to taste)

Version 2
¼ cup yogurt
2 tbsp Cajun spices (more or little to taste)

Combine ingredients either in a bowl or blender before pouring over your meat. This is especially good over chicken.

Sauces

Best BBQ Sauce EVER!

Okay, I know that is a very daring statement to make but I have been making this sauce for years and am yet to taste anything as good. My husband and friend built a hog spit a few years back and every time we roast a pig we use this, not as just the marinade but the sauce to go with the cooked pulled meat also. It is just delicious. There are a lot of ingredients but it is simple to make and stores really well.

Ingredients:
1 medium onion, peeled and quartered
10 cloves garlic, peeled
2 fresh red chillies, stalks removed
1 tbsp olive oil
10 sprigs fresh thyme – leaves removed
10 sprigs fresh rosemary - leaves removed
1 small bunch fresh cilantro
10 bay leaves
1 tsp cumin seeds
2 tbsp fennel seeds
2 tbsp smoked paprika

6 cloves
Zest and juice of 2 oranges
1 cup packed soft brown sugar
6 tbsp balsamic vinegar
1 ¾ cups tomato ketchup
2 tbsp Worcestershire sauce
2 tsp English mustard
1 ¾ cup apple juice
1 tsp sea salt
1 tsp freshly ground black pepper

1. Put the onion, chillies and garlic in to a food processor and whizz until you have a kind of paste.
2. Pour the olive in to a pan and put on a low - medium heat, add the onion mixture, turn the heat down to low and cook for around 5 minutes.
3. Next add all the herbs and spices to the food processor with the zest of the orange. Whizz until smooth then add to the pan with the onions.
4. Add the sugar and stir until it becomes a brown-ish paste then add a cup of water and cook for two minutes.
5. Add the juice of the oranges and turn the heat up, bring to the boil before lowering the heat and leaving to simmer for ten minutes or until the mixture has thickened.
6. Pour the sauce through a sieve in to a clean bowl, rinse the sieve and repeat so you get a really smooth sauce.
7. Leave to cool before using as a marinade.

BBQ TIP: If you wish to store the sauce - pour in to sterilised jars, put on the lids and then place the jars in to a pan of boiling water for 8-10 minutes. Remove and store in a dark place for up to 6 months, I guarantee it won't last that long though!

Homemade Ketchup

Delicious with burgers, sausages and of course chips! This homemade version is not full of sugar like some store bought varieties.

Ingredients:
1 tbsp olive oil
1oz butter
1 small yellow onion – finely chopped
1 clove of garlic – crushed
1-2 tsp Italian mixed herbs
2 large beef tomatoes – roughly chopped
½ cup tomato paste
2 tsp balsamic vinegar
Sea salt and black pepper to taste

1. Heat the oil and butter in a pan, then add the onion, garlic and dried herbs.
2. Cook for 3-4 minutes on a low-medium heat.
3. Stir in the tomatoes, tomato paste and balsamic vinegar.
4. Cook for a further 4-5 minutes then remove from the heat.
5. Pour in to a blender and whizz until you have a smooth sauce.
6. Taste for seasoning.

Chili BBQ Sauce

This is a great addition to those who like a little heat on their burger or hot dog. Using the homemade BBQ sauce in this book you can quickly whip this up in no time.

Ingredients:
1oz butter
1 tsp ground cumin
½ tsp ground cilantro (coriander)
½ tsp paprika
1 tsp chili powder
1/3 cup homemade BBQ sauce
2 tsp Worcestershire sauce

Heat the butter in a small saucepan and add the spices, cook for 30 seconds before stirring in the chili powder, homemade BBQ sauce and Worcestershire sauce. Remove from the heat and mix well.

Easy Peasy Homemade Mayo

As mayonnaise is the basis to a lot of sauces you cannot go wrong making your own. It really is so easy and tastes so much better.

Ingredients:
1 large free range egg
1 tbsp Dijon mustard
1 1/3 cups olive oil
4 tsp white wine vinegar
Sea salt and freshly ground black pepper to taste

Place the egg and mustard in to a food processor and whizz until smooth. With the motor running add the oil in slowly until combined. Add in the white wine vinegar and pulse until combined and smooth. Season to taste. Viola you now have homemade mayo. You can now make the following with this sauce as the base:

- Garlic Mayo
- Thousand Island dressing
- Marie Rose
- Aioli
- Tartare Sauce
- Horseradish
- Chili Mayo
- Mustard Mayo

Dry Rubs

Smokey Rib Rub

This is the prefect rub for pork ribs you want to smoke. Leave to infuse for 24-48 hours and smoke slowly for at least 4 hours but up to 8, depending on how you like your meat.

Ingredients:
1/3 cup sea salt (it HAS to be sea salt)
½ cup white sugar
½ cup packed brown sugar
2 tbsp garlic powder
2 tbsp onion powder
2 tbsp smoked paprika
3 tbsp hot red chili powder
2 tbsp ground black pepper
2 tsp cayenne pepper
2 tbsp dried thyme
1 tbsp dried rosemary
1 tbsp ground nutmeg
1 tbsp ground allspice

Mix all ingredients together in a bowl. Store at room temperature in an air tight container. To use rub all over meat and allow at least 24 hours before smoking. You can use this on meat to slow cook in the oven too. Slow cook for at least 4 hours on a low temperature so the sugar doesn't burn and the spices all cook in to the meat and mellow somewhat in taste.

Cajun Rub

It is very easy to make your own Cajun seasoning. This is the most used seasoning in my kitchen not just for BBQ season, but all year round!

Ingredients:
¼ cup coarse sea salt
¼ cup paprika
1 tbsp dried thyme
1 tbsp dried oregano
1 tbsp coarse black pepper
1 tbsp onion powder
1 tbsp garlic flakes (or powder)
2 tsp cayenne pepper
2 bay leaves – ground up

Combine all ingredients and grind a bit more in a pestle and mortar if required.
Add more cayenne if you like it hotter like us! Rub on your favorite meat, allow to stand for an hour to maximize flavor.

Mustard Rub

This is really good for any type of pork - tenderloin, chops, ribs and sausages. I also love this on chicken.

Ingredients:
7 tbsp dry mustard
3 tbsp dried oregano
2 tbsp chili powder
1 tbsp fresh ground pepper
1 tbsp garlic powder
1 tbsp onion powder

Mix all ingredients together and store in an airtight bag or container until required.

Cocoa Loco Rub

Wow this is one of those rubs that completely changes how to feel about ribs. I love ribs with BBQ sauce and sticky honey, actually, I like them with almost any rub or sauce but this one is outstanding. Everyone goes crazy for this at our BBQ's. You will not be disappointed.

Ingredients:
¼ cup unsweetened cocoa powder
½ cup light brown sugar
3 tbsp ancho powder
2 tbsp kosher salt
2 tbsp onion powder
1 tbsp granulated garlic
1 tbsp dried oregano
1 tbsp cayenne pepper
1 tbsp mustard powder
2 tsp ginger powder
2 tsp ground cinnamon
1 tsp ground allspice

Mix all ingredients together. When using, rub all over your ribs, wrap in plastic wrap and refrigerate overnight.

BBQ Rub

The original BBQ rub. It goes well with everything type of meat, poultry and fish.

Ingredients:
2 ½ tbsp dark brown sugar
2 tbsp paprika
2 tsp mustard powder
2 tsp onion powder
2 tsp garlic powder
1 ½ tsp dried basil
2 bay leaves - ground
¾ tsp ground coriander seed
¾ tsp ground savory
¾ tsp dried thyme
¾ tsp ground black pepper
¾ tsp ground white pepper
1/8 tsp ground cumin
Sea salt to taste

Combine all ingredients together and use to flavour any meats before BBQ or grilling, allowing them to sit in the rub overnight if possible, or at least two hours.

Burgers & Sausages

Homemade Beef Burgers

My best ever recipe for beef burgers is a simple but very tasty one. I know claiming your burgers are the best ever is a bit extravagant but I have yet to meet a single person who hasn't loved them. And of course they go great with the best ever BBQ sauce recipe at the start of the book. These can be prepared in advance and stored in the fridge for up to 24 hours or shaped and frozen.

Prep Time: 20 minutes + 30 minutes refrigeration
Cook Time: 25 minutes
Serves: 6

Ingredients:
2lb minced beef (I like to use minced steak)
1 small onion - finely chopped
1 egg – lightly beaten (you might not need the entire egg)
1-2 tbsp Cajun spices
½ tsp garlic powder
To dress the burgers
6 slices of cheddar cheese
2 large onions – cut in to slices
6 wholemeal baps
6 large lettuce leaves - chopped
1 large beef tomato – sliced
Homemade mustard mayo & BBQ sauce (at the start of the book)

Method
1. Place the mince, onion, spices and garlic in to a bowl and mix well to combine. Add a half of the egg and combine. If it feels the right consistency shape in to 6 equal burger patties around half an inch thick.
2. Place the burgers on to the center of a hot oiled BBQ rack and cook for 8 minutes on each side topping each one with cheddar cheese for the last minute or two.
3. Assemble the burgers by adding the mustard mayo to the bottom of the baps and top with the lettuce. Next add your burger, top with onions and homemade BBQ sauce top with other half of the bap. Mmmmm

Lamb & Feta Burgers

These burgers have become a staple in our house all year round. In the winter I fry them in a griddle pan and serve them with stem broccoli and spicy baby potatoes.

Prep Time: 30 minutes
Cook Time: 10-15 minutes
Makes: 8 patties

Ingredients:
2lb good quality minced lamb
1 small onion – chopped finely
8oz feta – crumbled
1 tbsp freshly chopped mint
1 clove garlic – crushed

Method:
1. Place all the ingredients in to a food processor and whizz until all the ingredients are combined. This will not take long.
2. Remove the mixture from the food processor and shape in to 8 even patties.
3. Cook on a hot BBQ, a hot flat plate or an oiled rack. Cook for 5 minutes each side or until they are cooked through.
4. Serve in buns with a spice tomato sauce or salsa.

Chicken Fillet Burger with Lemon & Garlic Mayo

These can be served in a bun or with a salad, they are very versatile. The chicken can be marinated and left up to a day before.

Prep Time: 20 minutes + 3 hours marinade time
Cook Time: 15-20 minutes
Serves: 4

Ingredients:
4 chicken breast fillets
½ cup fresh lime juice
1 tbsp sweet chili sauce
½ cup natural yogurt
4 smoked rashers of bacon
4 hamburger buns
4 large lettuce leaves

Method
1. Combine the yogurt, lime juice and sweet chili sauce in a bowl.
2. Put the chicken breasts in to a dish and punch holes in to each breast with a sharp knife tip. Pour over the yogurt mixture then cover and allow to marinate for at least 3 hours, overnight if you can.

3. Remove excess marinade from the chicken breasts before adding to a hot BBQ for 10 minutes before adding the bacon. Cook for 5 minutes until the chicken is golden and cooked through.
4. To make the lemon & garlic mayo add 2 cloves crushed garlic and one tablespoon of lemon juice to my homemade mayo at the start of the book.
5. Assemble the burger by toasting the burger buns, adding the lettuce, chicken, bacon and topping with some tangy mayo before putting the lid on and devouring!

Chili Beef Burger

For those of you who like a nice kick to a burger this will definitely satisfy your taste buds. The chili I use in my recipe will give a spicy burger, if you prefer it a little milder just reduce the amount of chili by a teaspoon or two.

Prep Time: 25 minutes
Cook Time: 10 minutes
Serves: 6

Ingredients:
1kg good quality minced beef
1 small onion – finely chopped
3 tsp fresh chopped red chili
1 tsp ground cumin
2 tbsp tomato paste
2 tbsp freshly chopped cilantro
6 floury baps
6 lettuce leaves
Tomato and onion salsa
2 beef tomatoes – chopped
1 small onion – chopped
1 tsp lime juice
1 tsp olive oil
Sea salt & freshly ground pepper to taste

Method
1. Place the mince in to a large mixing bowl with the onion, cumin, chili, tomato paste and cilantro. Mix well using your hands then shape in to 6 even patties.
2. Cook on a hot BBQ grill or flat plate for 4 minutes each side.
3. Serve in the floury baps with lettuce and top with the salsa.

Homemade Jumbo Pork Sausages with Mustard Cream

Quick and easy to prepare these homemade jumbo sausages can be prepared in advance and stored you your fridge until ready to cook. They are versatile too, so feel free to add herbs and spices to change it up!

Prep Time: 20 minutes
Cook Time: 15 minutes
Serves: 6

Ingredients:
2lb good quality pork mince
1 small onion – chopped finely
1 cup stale breadcrumbs
2 garlic cloves – crushed
1 egg – whisked lightly
1 tsp dried sage
6 crusty bread rolls

Mustard Cream
½ cup sour cream
1 tbsp wholegrain or French mustard
2 tsp lemon juice

Method:
1. Place the minced pork, onion, garlic, breadcrumbs, sage and egg in to a large mixing bowl and combine well with your hands. Divide in to 6 equal jumbo sausage shaped patties.
2. Cook for 5-10 minutes on a hot lightly oiled BBQ grill or flatplate, turning frequently.
3. To make the mustard cream mix all ingredients together in a small bowl.
4. Once the jumbo sausages are cooked, place in to the roll and dollop with mustard cream.

Oozy Cheese Burger

These burgers are stuffed with cheese so it oozes out when you bite in. You can use any cheese you like - I have tried it with cheddar, brie, Roquefort, feta and goats' cheese. It was fantastic with every one of them! I also like to serve these in buns with gherkins and homemade ketchup.

Prep Time: 25 minutes
Cook Time: 20 minutes
Serves: 6

Ingredients:
2lbs beef mince
1 small onion – finely chopped
2 tbsp freshly chopped parsley
1 tsp dried oregano
1 tbsp Cajun spices
3oz cheddar cheese – cut in to 6 even squares
6 burger buns
6 lettuce leaves
Gherkins – sliced
Homemade ketchup

Method:
1. In a large mixing bowl combine the mince, onion, herbs and Cajun spices. Shape in to 6 even burgers.
2. With your thumb make a small hole in the center of each burger, not going the entire way through. Add a square of cheese and cover back over so the cheese is completely covered.
3. Cook on your BBQ for 4-5 minutes each side. To serve place the lettuce in the bottom of each bun, top with the burger then gherkins and some ketchup.

Hotdogs with Coleslaw

The good old BBQ favorite. These ones are a little different as they have a lovely homemade slaw in the roll for crunch and creaminess.

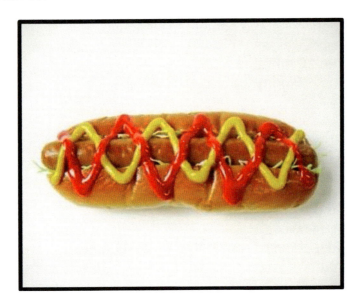

Prep Time: 20 minutes
Cook Time: 10 minutes
Serves: 6

Ingredients:
6 large Frankfurt sausages
1 tbsp oil
6 hot dog rolls
6 lettuce leaves – chopped
Coleslaw
½ head red cabbage
½ head green cabbage
2 scallions (spring onions)
1 small white onion – sliced
½ cup homemade mayo
1 tbsp German mustard

Method:

1. Slice the sausages three or four times cutting about half way through. Brush each with a little oil and cook for 8-10 minutes on the BBQ grill or flat plate.
2. To make the coleslaw add all the ingredients together and mix well to combine.
3. To serve cut through the rolls lengthways and add the lettuce. Top with creamy coleslaw and then add the sizzling hotdog.

Optional: drizzle with ketchup and American mustard

Honey Soy Sausages

These sausages are super sticky and tasty as they are left to marinate overnight. Please make sure you get good quality sausages that are pure pork and not full of fat. Your butcher will probably be the best place to get them. This marinade is great over chicken, lamb and beef too!

Prep Time: 15 minutes + marinating time
Cook Time: 5-6 minutes
Serves: 4

Ingredients:
8-10 good quality thick butcher style pork sausages
1" piece of fresh root ginger – peeled and grated finely
1/3 cup soy sauce
1/3 cup organic honey
1 clove garlic – crushed
2 sprigs fresh thyme – leaves removed

Method
1. Put the sausages in to a large dish.
2. In a smaller bowl add the ginger, honey, soy, garlic and thyme whisk to combine and pour over the sausages, cover and allow to marinade overnight.
3. Place on a lightly greased barbeque grill.
4. Cook the sausages for 5-6 minutes basting regularly with the leftover marinade. The sausages will be sticky from the marinade.

Finger Lickin' Chicken

Sweet and Sticky Chicken Breasts

I have yet to meet anyone who doesn't like some sticky chicken at a BBQ, be it a chicken wing, thigh, drumstick or breast. These can be served as a main course dish along with some homemade crispy potato wedges and a tossed salad.

Prep Time: 6 minutes + 20 minutes marinating
Cook Time: 10 minutes
Serves: 6

Ingredients:
8 chicken breasts (5-6oz each) – skin removed, trimmed of any fat and sinew
2 oz butter - softened
¼ cup organic honey
¼ cup homemade bbq sauce
2 tsp wholegrain mustard

Method:

1. Makes slashes on each chicken breast with a sharp knife, 3-4 will do.
2. Mix together the bbq sauce, honey, butter and mustard and slather on to the chicken breasts. You should have half the marinade leftover to baste while cooking.
3. Put the chicken breasts on to a hot BBQ cut side down and cook for 3-4 minutes each side until cooked through, brushing with extra marinade while cooking. Serve hot

Tandoori Chicken Skewers

Tandoori chicken skewers using out spiced yogurt marinade from the start of the book. These are so juicy, tender and tasty. Make sure to make extra as they always run out early!

Prep Time: 20 minutes + marinating time 3 – 24 hours
Cook Time: 10 minutes
Serves: 4-6

Ingredients:
4-6 chicken breast – cut in to long strips (you can use thigh meat here if you prefer)
Spiced yogurt recipe (full recipe)

Method
1. Place the chicken strips in to a bowl and add the marinade. Allow to marinade for a few hours or overnight.
2. Skewer the chicken on to wooden or metal skewers. If using wooden make sure to soak for 20 minutes in cold water before add the chicken to stop them burning.
3. Place the skewers on to a hot BBQ and cook for 8-10 minutes or until cooked through and tender.

BBQ Chicken Thighs

Thighs are my favorite when cooked on a BBQ. I love the charring of the skin edges and with our homemade BBQ sauce, these will go down an absolute treat.

Prep Time: 20 minutes
Cook Time: 35-40 minutes
Serves: 4

Ingredients:
1 cup & ¼ homemade BBQ sauce
8 chicken thighs, bones removed

Method
1. Place thighs in to a large bowl and cover with half the marinade, we will use the rest to base them throughout cooking.
2. Place chicken thighs on to a medium BBQ, at the edges of the BBQ is where I cook mine.
3. Allow to cook for 10-12 minutes basting with more marinade then turn and cook for the same on the other side. I allow another 5-10 minutes cooking time, or longer if needed.
4. Always check to make sure the thighs are cooked before serving, as the thigh meat is darker it will remain slightly pink when cooked.

Cajun Chicken Kebabs

What I love about chicken kebabs is you can add whatever you prefer, there's no rule. I love to change it up and add cherry tomatoes, chunks of red onion and red bell pepper. Other times I will add eggplant, zucchini and sweet potato chunks. It really is up to you, they are extremely versatile. I use the Cajun marinade here but you can easily use garlic and lemon.

Prep Time: 25 minutes + marinating time for chicken
Cook Time: 10 minutes
Serves: 4

Ingredients:
4 chicken breasts – cut in to 6-8 even chunks per breast
2 red onion – cut in to 6 chunks each
12 cherry tomatoes
1 yellow bell pepper
4 tbsp Cajun marinade (from start of book)

Method
1. Place the chicken chunks in to a bowl and add the marinade. Leave to infuse for anything up to 24 hours.

2. Thread the chicken and vegetables on to wooden or metal skewers. If using wooden ensure you have soaked them for at least 20 minutes in cold water to prevent burning.
3. Place the kebabs on to a hot BBQ grill or flat plate and cook for 10 minutes or until cooked through, turning occasionally to ensure even cooking.

Buffalo Chicken Wings with Ranch Dressing

As is traditional, I deep-fry these wings first before marinating with the sauce and leaving to infuse all those amazing buffalo flavors before cooking on the BBQ the next day - serve with a yummy homemade ranch dressing or a spicy chili sauce.

Prep Time: 25 minutes + marinating time of 3-24hours
Cook Time: 10 minutes
Serves: 4

Ingredients:
2lb large chicken wings
2 tsp freshly ground black pepper
2 tsp onion powder
2 tsp garlic salt
½ cup homemade tomato sauce
2 tbsp Worcestershire sauce
1oz butter melted
2 tsp brown sugar
Few shakes tabasco sauce
Olive oil – to deep fry

Ranch dressing

½ cup homemade mayonnaise
½ cup sour cream
2 tbsp fresh lemon juice
2 tbsp freshly chopped chives
Sea salt & freshly ground black pepper to taste

Method
1. To prepare the wings cut the tip off each chicken wing. Snap each wing at the joint then cut through the joint to give you two chicken pieces.
2. Mix the peppers, onion powder and garlic salt together then rub in to each wing.
3. Heat the olive oil to medium-high heat in a heavy based pan and deep fry the chicken pieces in batches for around 2 minutes. Remove and drain on paper.
4. Put the chicken pieces in to a large shallow dish.
5. Mix all remaining ingredients together then pour over the chicken, stirring to ensure all the pieces are covered.
6. Cover the dish and place in the fridge for 3-24 hours.
7. To BBQ place the chicken pieces on to a lightly oiled BBQ grill or hot flat plate. Cook for 5-7 minutes, basting with more marinade throughout.
8. To make the ranch dressing mix all the ingredients together.
9. Serve immediately.

Garlic and Lemon Drummers

Drumsticks are the ultimate BBQ food as they can be held in your hand, albeit not for long as they are munched up super quick with this garlic and lemon marinade from the start of the book.

Prep Time: 20 minutes + 3 hours marinating time
Cook Time: 20 minutes
Serves: 4

Ingredients:
8 chicken drumsticks
1 cup of garlic and lemon marinade (in marinades)

Method:
1. Trim off any extra fat and sinew from the drumsticks. Score the drumsticks 3 or 4 times with a sharp knife before putting in to a shallow dish. Pour over the marinade over the drumsticks, ensuring they are all covered. Allow to infuse for at least 3 hours or overnight.
2. Before cooking drain off the marinade, reserving to baste while cooking.
3. Cook for 15-20 minutes on a hot BBQ.
4. Serve immediately.

Lamb, Beef & Pork

BBQ Spare Ribs

A BBQ isn't a BBQ without succulent ribs! Tender, tasty and falling off the bone – perfect!

Prep Time: 15 minutes + at least 3 hours marinating
Cook Time: 30 minutes
Serves: 4-6

Ingredients:
2lb American style pork spare ribs
3 cups homemade BBQ sauce

Method:
1. Trim the ribs of sinew and excess fat before cutting in to pieces where each piece has 4 ribs.
2. Heat the BBQ sauce in a large saucepan and bring to the boil. Reduce the heat to a simmer before adding in the rib pieces. Cook on a low heat with the lid on for 15-20 minutes stirring occasionally to ensure all ribs cook evenly.
3. Pour the ribs and sauce in to a large dish and cool. Once cooled cover and refrigerate for 3-24 hours.

4. To cook place ribs on a hot BBQ for 15 minutes, basting with the sauce as you cook. I love these with my crunchy potato salad (in salads & sides)

Peppered Steaks

No marinating involved so these are quick. Just heat the BBQ and off you go! Serve with homemade giant wedges. I like to serve these with horseradish sauce but garlic mayo is just as nice.

Prep Time: 15 minutes
Cook Time: 10 minutes
Serves: 4

Ingredients:
4 medium sirloin steaks (8-10oz each)
¼ cup mixed cracked pepper (I use red, pink & black peppercorns & crush myself)

Method:
1. Lightly oil each side of the steaks before pressing the peppercorn mixture on to both sides.
2. Cook the steaks on a hot BBQ fir 5 -10 minutes, depending on how you like them cooked. I have mine medium rare so cook for roughly 3 minutes per side.

Herby Lamb Cutlets

My favorite meat of all time is lamb, especially lamb cutlets as when cooked right the meat just melts in your mouth. They only take 6-8 minutes to cook on a hot BBQ too, a homemade mint jelly goes perfectly with these.

Prep Time: 15 minutes + 20 minutes marinating
Cook Time: 6-8 minutes
Serves: 4

Ingredients:
12 good quality lamb cutlets – trimmed
2-3 sprigs of rosemary leaves – chopped finely
2 tbsp olive oil
1 tsp freshly ground black pepper

Method:
1. Put the lamb cutlets in to a shallow bowl and drizzle over half the oil, then add half the rosemary and black pepper and rub in using your hands. Turn over and repeat with the remaining oil, rosemary and pepper.
2. Place on a hot BBQ and cook for 3-4 minutes each side until pink in the center.
3. Serve immediately

Cocoa Loco Ribs

As I mentioned at the start of the book in the cocoa loco rub recipe, everyone goes ape for ribs when I have this rub on them. Smokey and tangy, you're going to love these. I pre-cook in the oven first before finishing on a hot BBQ for the perfect taste.

Prep Time: 10 minutes + marinating time
Cook Time: 1hr 30 minutes
Serves: 8

Ingredients:
4lb baby back ribs
Cocoa loco rub recipe

Method:
1. Rub marinade all over the ribs and leave to marinade for at least 3 hours up to 24.
2. Pre-heat oven to 350F / 180C and bake for 1 hour.
3. Transfer ribs to a medium hot BBQ and cook for 20 – 25 minutes. You can baste with some homemade BBQ sauce while cooking on the BBQ. Cut in to portions and serve immediately.

Mustard rubbed Pork Loin Chops

These chops can be grilled as well as barbequed. They make a great mid-week dinner and can be left to marinate overnight. Serve with homemade apple sauce or chutney.

Prep Time: 20 minutes + 3 hours marinating
Cook Time: 16-20 minutes
Serves: 6

Ingredients:
6 pork loin chops
2-3 tbsp mustard rub

Method:
1. Press the mustard rub in to each chop to ensure they are all covered. If leaving to infuse cover dish and place in the fridge.
2. To cook place chops on a hot BBQ grill or flat plate. Cook for 6-8 minutes each side until cooked through and tender.
3. Serve immediately with some apple chutney or sauce.

Seafood

Garlic King Prawns

We use our chili and lime marinade from the marinades section at the start of the book for this recipe. Another simple marinade is just lemon juices, sesame oil, garlic and ginger. Kind prawns cook so quickly and make a great snack while waiting for the remaining meats to cook.

Prep Time: 5 minutes + marinating time
Cook Time: 5 minutes
Serves: 6

Ingredients:
1lb king prawns – heads removed, deveined and peeled
Chili & Lime marinade from start of book

Method
1. Marinade the prawns for 15minutes before placing on to wooden skewers and pour over any remaining marinade.
2. Cook on a hot flatplate of lightly oiled BBQ grill. Cook for 3-5 minutes or until cooked through and pink in color.
3. Serve immediately.

Perfect Fish Patties

You can use any firm white fish for these like whiting, cod, hake, perch or pollock. They go great with a tossed salad and some easy peasy homemade mayo from the sauce section. Add some capers, chives and parsley to the mayo, this will being out the flavors of the fish.

Prep Time: 25 minutes
Cook Time: 10 minutes
Serves: 8-10 burgers / patties

Ingredients:
1 1/2lbs white fish fillets – cubed
3 scallions – chopped
1 cup stale white breadcrumbs
¼ cup lemon juice
1 tbsp freshly chopped dill
2 tbsp freshly chopped parsley
1 egg
¾ cup grated cheddar cheese (I like a mature variety)
½ cup plain flour – for dusting

Method:
1. Put the fish cubes in to a food processor and whizz for about 20 seconds until smooth. Place the fish then in to a bowl with the breadcrumbs, lemon juice, scallions. Herbs, egg and cheese. Combine all the ingredients together so they are well mixed.
2. Shape in to 8-10 even size patties, place on a baking sheet and refrigerate for 15 minutes.
3. Place the flour on a plate, cover each pattie with flour then shake the excess off before cooing on a hot BBQ flatplate for 2-3 minutes before turning and cooking for the same on the other side.
4. Serve with some feta salad and herby mayonnaise.

Bream & Vegetable Parcels

These parcels only take 10 minutes to cook and are so easy to prepare. You can even make ahead and store in the fridge for several hours before cooking. You can also use different vegetables like zucchini and carrot. The fish stays extremely moist as it steams in the parcel.

Prep Time: 15 minutes
Cook Time: 10 minutes
Serves: 4

Ingredients:
4 bream fillets
2 tbsp horseradish cream
1 small tomato – diced finely
4oz can corn kernels – drained
2/3 cup grated cheddar cheese (red or white)
½ red bell pepper – diced finely
1 celery stick – diced finely
3 scallions – chopped
1 ½ tsp dried mixed herbs
Sea salt & freshly ground black pepper to taste

Method:
1. Lightly spray 4 sheets of foil about double the length of the fillets
2. Place a fillet of fish on to the centre of each piece of foil and spread a quarter of the horseradish cream on to each fillet.
3. Top each piece of fish with the chopped vegetables, herbs and season to taste.
4. To make the parcel bring the foil edges together and seal by folding.
5. Place the parcels fish-side down on to a hot BBQ grill or flatplate and cook for 6 minutes. Check to see if the fish is cooked, if it flakes easily and has turned opaque it is cooked.

6. Serve immediately with a baked potato and tossed salad.

Balsamic Salmon

This salmon is perfect served with baby BBQ baked potatoes and some charred broccoli stems.

Prep Time: 10 minutes (+ 2 hours marinating)
Cook Time: 10 minutes
Serves: 4

Ingredients:
4 x 4oz salmon fillets
¼ cup lemon juice
Sea salt to taste
2 tbsp balsamic vinegar
1 clove garlic – crushed
3 tbsp olive oil
1 sprig rosemary

Method
1. Place all ingredients apart from salmon in to a blender and whizz.
2. Place salmon fillets in to a shallow dish and pour over the marinade. Cover and refrigerate for 1-2 hours.
3. Remove the salmon fillets from the marinade and shake off any excess. Place on a hot BBQ grill or flatplate for 4 minutes each side, or until cooked through and flaking.

Vegetables, Salads & Sides

Chickpea Salad

You can use tinned or dried chickpeas for this salad. If using dried you will need to soak overnight before cooking. This is a really fresh salad and goes well with all meats, especially chicken.

Prep Time: 20 minutes (overnight is using dried chickpeas)
Cook Time: if using dried 30-40 minutes
Serves: 6-8

Ingredients:
2 large cans of chickpeas – drained
¼ cup olive oil
1 red onion – sliced
3 beef tomatoes – de-seeded and cut in to small dice
1 small red bell pepper – sliced in long strips
3 scallions (spring onions) – cut in to long strips
1 cup freshly chopped parsley
3 tbsp freshly chopped mint

Tahini Dressing
2 tbsp tahini paste
2 tbsp water

¼ cup olive oil
2 tbsp fresh lemon juice
2 garlic cloves – crushed
½ tsp ground cumin
Sea salt & freshly ground black pepper

Method
1. Place chickpeas, sliced onion, chopped tomatoes, red pepper, scallions and herbs in to a large bowl, mix well.
2. Add all dressing ingredients in to a jar and shake well to combine.
3. Pour dressing over salad and mix through to ensure all ingredients are covered.

Tomato & Potato Bake

Layers of potato and tomato with herbs and topped with cheddar make this side a wonderful veggie main course too.

Prep Time: 15 minutes
Cook Time: 1hr 15 minutes
Serves: 8 as side dish

Ingredients:
8 medium potatoes – thinly sliced
2oz melted butter
1 tbsp mixed fresh herbs – thyme, rosemary & parsley
Sea salt and freshly ground black pepper
1 ¼ cups cream
2 ripe beef tomatoes – sliced
1 cup cheddar – grated
1 tbsp fresh chives - chopped

Method:
1. Preheat oven to 350F / 180C. Brush a shallow baking dish with the melted butter and place in the sliced potatoes arranging in a circle and layering, so the overlap.
2. Season with salt and pepper, sprinkle over the herbs and pour the cream in to the middle of the dish.
3. Cover the dish with foil and bake in the center of your oven for an hour.
4. Remove potatoes from the oven and turn the heat up to 420F / 210C.
5. Add the sliced tomatoes over the potatoes then sprinkle over the cheddar. Place back in to the oven for 15 minutes or until the cheese has started to go golden.
6. Scatter over the chives and serve.

Not so traditional Coleslaw

The reason I say this is not traditional is there is no cabbage in this. Of course you can add cabbage to this but I started making this as I rarely have cabbage in the house. The red onion and carrot mixed with homemade mayonnaise is crunchy and fresh. I sometimes use Greek yogurt instead of the mayo too.

Prep Time: 10 minutes
Cook Time: 0
Serves: 6-8 as a side

Ingredients:
3 large organic carrots (I use ones from my vegetable patch) - grated
2 red onion - sliced
3-4 tbsp homemade mayo (depending on how creamy you like it)
2 scallions (spring onions) chopped
Handful fresh parsley - chopped

Method
1. Place all ingredients in to a bowl and combine until you get the consistency you like. Add more mayo if that's how you like it.

Crispy Bacon & Potato Salad – two ways

I make this potato salad two ways, depending on my mood really. The first way is more of a traditional one including crispy bacon. The second one is all crispy – potatoes and bacon and baked in the oven.

Prep Time: 20 minutes
Cook Time: 10 minutes
Serves: 8

Ingredients:
3lb red potatoes (roosters) – cut in 1" pieces
Medium red onion – sliced
3 slices of bacon – chopped
¾ cup plain yogurt
¾ cup homemade mayonnaise
3 scallions – chopped

Method 1:

1. Put the potatoes in to a saucepan and cover with boiling water, cook until tender then drain and allow to cool in a large missing bowl.

2. Cook the bacon lardons in a pan until they are crispy, drain on kitchen towel and add to the potatoes.
3. Mix the mayo, spring onions and yogurt in a small bowl. Add the sliced onion to the mixing bowl along with the mayo mix and gently fold it all together.

Method 2:

1. Preheat oven to 350F / 180C
2. This method uses just the potatoes and bacon. Cube the potatoes and place in the oven for 20 minutes. Turn the heat up to 400F / 200C and add the chopped bacon for 10-15 minutes until the potatoes and bacon are golden and crispy. Shake a sprig of rosemary over just before serving.

Feta Salad

Full of fresh vegetables, olives and crumbly Feta cheese, this salad is a light accompaniment to BBQ meats. This is also lovely with the addition of char grilled bell peppers through it.

Prep Time: 5 minutes
Serves: 4-6

Ingredients:
1 tbsp olive oil
4 beef tomatoes - roughly chopped in to large dice
½ English cucumber - large dice
Handful pitted black olives
4oz / 100g feta cheese – cut in to cubes
Handful fresh basil leaves
Splash balsamic vinegar

Method:
Place the tomatoes, cucumber, olives and feta in to a large bowl. Tear the basil leaves with your hands and sprinkle over the salad. Whisk the oil and vinegar together then drizzle over. Serve!

Corn on the Cob with Tomato Relish

What's a BBQ without corn on the cob! Every child's favorite part. This one is served with a tangy tomato relish that can be put on burgers, served with chops and with melted cheese. It's very versatile.

Prep Time: 15 minutes
Cook Time: 1 hour
Serves: 6

Ingredients:
6 large fresh cobs of corn
2 tbsp olive oil
2oz butter
Sea salt – to taste

Tomato Relish
1 x 14oz can chopped plum tomatoes
2/3 cup white vinegar
1 clove garlic – crushed
½ cup white sugar
2 scallions – chopped finely
4 sun-dried tomatoes – chopped finely

1 fresh red chili (small) – chopped finely
½ tsp sea salt
Freshly ground black pepper – to taste

Method:
1. To make the relish whizz the tomatoes in a food processor. Add the vinegar and sugar to a medium size saucepan and place on a medium heat. When the sugar has dissolved bring it to the boil before reducing the sauce to a simmer.
2. Add in the garlic, spring onions, sun-dried tomatoes, chili and chopped tomatoes, bring up to the boil before reducing to a simmer and cook for 35 minutes, stirring every few minutes.
3. Season with sea salt and black pepper and cook until the sauce has thickened, a further 5 minutes should do it. Remove from the heat and allow to cool.
4. Brush the corn cobs with the oil and cook on a hot BBQ grill for 4-5 minutes each side until the corn is cooked and charred brown in places. Remove to a serving dish and place a square of butter on each cob. Add extra salt if required and serve with tomato relish.

Cheesy Herby 'Shrooms

Any type of mushroom can be used for this recipe but I prefer the large field mushrooms. They do take longer to cook but they have hold more filling. You can use button or cup mushrooms also for smaller snacks.

Prep Time: 10 minutes
Cook Time: 5-6 minutes
Serves: 6

Ingredients:
6 large mushrooms (I use field)
2 oz melted butter
2 garlic cloves – crushed
1 tbsp fresh thyme leaves
2 tbsp fresh chives – chopped
½ cup parmesan – shredded finely

Method:
1. Peel the mushrooms and remove the stalks and set to one side.
2. In a bowl mix together the butter and garlic.
3. Brush the mushroom tops with the garlic butter and place open side down on to a hot BBQ flatplate. Cook for 2 minutes before turning over and brushing the inside with the garlic butter.
4. Sprinkle the bases of the mushrooms with the mixed herbs then add the parmesan. Cook for 3-4 minutes or until the cheese begins to melt then serve.

Conclusion

Some barbeques can be formal and used for a dinner parties and others can be informal and used for lunch at the beach. Whatever the case you now know the benefits of barbequing, the different types of barbeques and have recipes for marinades, rubs, sauces, meats, poultry, fish, salads and sides. It's time for you to light that barbeque and get cooking!

Happy eating folks!
Rob

Printed in Great Britain
by Amazon.co.uk, Ltd.,
Marston Gate.